Editions L.A.

DIGITAL CREATIVE AGENCY

We Transform Your Vision Into Creative Results

Editions L.A. is a full-service agency based in Los Angeles. Our company is a collective of amazing people striving to build delightful services
We believe that is all about getting your message across clearly and with a "Wow!" thrown in for good measure.

Our Awesome Services

Branding

We build, style and tone your brand identity from the ground up.
We rebrand established bands, brands or businesses.

Merchandise Store
Website design and E-Commerce
Website updates

Digital Marketing

CD Cover | Banners | Logo design | Flyers | Brochures |
Leaflets | Print ads | Magazine covers & artworks
Facebook / twitter / instagram / youtube artworks
| Book cover
Infographics | Icon Design |
| TshirtsProduct Labels | Presentation slides
Corporate graphics
Professional photo editing & enhancing
Redesign existing elements
YouTube Optimization and Monetization
Youtube Video Editing
Lyric Video and Advertising Design.

Publishing

BOOK COVER DESIGN
EBOOK FORMATTING SERVICES
and distribution on major platforms
(Amazon, Barnes & Nobles..)

Tell us about your dream and we will make it true!

Editions L.A.
7210 Jordan Avenue Suite B42, Canoga Park, California 91303, United States
info@edtions-la.com
Website: www.editions-la.com

Pump it up Magazine

TABLE OF CONTENTS

Letter from The Editor — 5
Anissa Sutton

SECRETS TO A LONG, HEALTHY LIFE — 11
- Dopamine Workouts
- 8 Chill Reads for Stress Relief
- Christian Songs to Ease Stress & Anxiety

WELLNESS — 21
8 Sleep Hacks for a Better You!

TOP NETFLIX — 30
Movies to Empower & Inspire

QUIZZ
Test Your Emotional Intelligence

CINDY DAVIS
Singing with Strength & Sharing God's Love

8 FASHION TIPS
For Old Money Vibes!

TRAVEL
In the Footsteps of Jesus: A Spiritual Journey Through the Holy Land

HUMANITARIAN AWARENESS
8 Ways to Help Stop the War and Support Those in Need

Reach for the Stars – While Standing on Earth!

Pump it up MAGAZINE ®

PUMP IT UP MAGAZINE
LINKS

WEBSITE
www.pumpitupmagazine.com

FACEBOOK
www.facebook.com/pumpitupmagazine

TWITTER
www.twitter.com/pumpitupmag

SOUNDCLOUD
www.soundcloud.com/pumpitupmagazine

INSTAGRAM
pumpitupmagazine

PINTEREST
www.pinterest.com/pumpitupmagazine

PUMP IT UP MAGAZINE
30721 Russell Ranch Road
Suite 140
Westlake Village,
California 91362
United States

 (818)514 – 0038(Ext:102)
 info@pumpitupmagazine.com

LETTER FROM THE EDITOR

Hey there, Pump It Up Family!

Welcome to the October edition of Pump It Up Magazine—the month when pumpkins are everywhere, the leaves start changing (at least for some of us!), and it feels like the perfect time for a fresh start. And trust me, this issue is all about it: faith, strength, and a big dose of empowerment.

I'm so excited to have Cindy Davis as our cover star this month. If you don't already know Cindy, you're in for a treat. This woman embodies resilience, faith, and the kind of patience that's truly inspiring (you know, the kind that makes you want to give your problems a serious side-eye).

Her new single, "Wait On You," drops in October 2028, and let me tell you—it's like a warm, soulful hug for anyone needing a reminder that God's timing is worth the wait.

But this issue isn't just about Cindy's story. We've packed it with tips to boost your well-being. Want to shake off stress? We've got dopamine workouts that'll make you smile and sweat. Need some quiet time? Check out our list of calming Christian songs that can turn down the noise in your head.

And if you're up for a spiritual adventure, take a trip with us "In the Footsteps of Jesus" through the Holy Land—it's a journey that could stir your soul without you even leaving the couch.

Let's not forget about the power of good stories and small acts of kindness. Our Humanitarian Awareness section highlights simple ways to support those impacted by war. Because, honestly, we all could use a little more compassion in the world right now, right?

So, grab your favorite drink, get cozy, and let's dive into October with a heart full of faith, a mind ready for inspiration, and maybe a few pumpkin-flavored snacks on hand. 😉

Thanks for sticking with us. Your support and enthusiasm mean the world, and I hope this issue brings you a little extra joy, hope, and maybe even a few good laughs.

Stay fabulous!

With love and lots of pumpkin spice,

Editor-in-Chief, Pump It Up Magazine

Anissa Sutton

CONTRIBUTORS

FOUNDER & EDITOR IN CHIEF
Anissa Boudjaoui Sutton

OWNERS
Anissa & Michael B. Sutton

MARKETING
Grace Rose
Anissa Sutton
Carter Kaya

DESIGN
Robert Afobi
Anissa Sutton

Cover magazine photo
www.AnissaSutton.com
Photography
EDITIONS-LA.COM

PARTNERS

Editions L.A.
www.editions-la.com

The Sound Of L.A.
www.thesoundofla.com

YMC
YourMusicConsultant.com

Info Music
www.infomusic.fr

*P.S. Did you know?
Pump It Up Magazine
is not only online
but also in print and digital,
distributed in more than
100 stores
through print-on-demand.
So, you can catch us
wherever you go!*

Cindy Davis

Interview with:
Cindy Davis
Empowerment Through Faith, Music, and Self-Growth

Cindy Davis Releases Debut Single "Wait On You"
A Soulful Gospel & Motown Fusion

Cindy Davis is a singer, broadcaster, and founder of CinDav Productions whose story is filled with both heartache and triumph. Through her faith, Cindy has found strength in moments when life seemed unbearable, reminding us all that it's never too late to pursue our dreams.

A Story of Loss and Hope
Cindy has endured profound losses, including the passing of her mother and stepfather within three months, followed by the loss of her younger sister. These events shook her to the core. Yet, she leaned on her faith, prayer, and Gospel music to find healing. "All things work together for good" is her guiding belief, a powerful reminder that even in the darkest times, God is at work.

Turning Setbacks into Comebacks
Life threw more challenges her way, from financial struggles—like being unable to afford a new car after hers broke down—to being unexpectedly fired from a toxic job as a dental assistant. These setbacks could have stopped her, but Cindy chose to see them as opportunities for growth. She recalls learning from life coach Tim Story that "setbacks are set-ups for comebacks."

The Heart of Her Music: "Wait On You"
Cindy's latest single, "Wait On You," is a testament to trusting God's timing. It's more than a song; it's a heartfelt message for anyone feeling lost, reminding them that patience and faith can lead to unexpected blessings. Blending Gospel warmth with Motown soul, it's Cindy's way of saying, "Keep going—God's got you." Produced by Michael B. Sutton, a legendary former Motown producer, the song carries an uplifting vibe that Cindy hopes will touch the hearts of listeners everywhere.

Empowering Women Through Faith
Empowering others, especially women, is at the heart of Cindy's mission. Through CinDav Productions and her work in women's ministry, she's inspired countless women to rise above challenges, guided by faith and determination. Cindy's interviews with legends like The Jacksons, Freda Payne, and Denise Matthews have taught her that resilience is key, and she shares this message through her music and outreach.

Looking Ahead
Cindy's vision is simple: spread hope, love, and wisdom to as many people as possible. She's living proof that it's never too late to embrace your calling, and her music serves as a beacon for those navigating tough times.

So, when you listen to "Wait On You," remember—no matter where you are in life, it's never too late to start again. Keep getting up, keep moving forward, and always trust the process.

Cindy Davis

PUMP IT UP MAGAZINE: How has your faith shaped your career?

CINDY DAVIS: Faith guides every step. For example, God once led me to work at McDonald's, where I helped a young man on his spiritual journey. Moments like this show me that my career is built on purpose and grace.

PUMP IT UP MAGAZINE: How does music empower women and share the Word of God?

CINDY DAVIS: Music inspires, uplifts, and spreads hope, allowing me to empower women and share messages of resilience and faith.

PUMP IT UP MAGAZINE: Tell us about your new single, "Wait On You."

CINDY DAVIS: It's a song about patience, resilience, and trusting God's timing, blending gospel warmth with Motown soul.

PUMP IT UP MAGAZINE: Why do you share uplifting messages on social media?

CINDY DAVIS: In chaotic times, hope is needed more than ever. Sharing the Word of God brings light to others' lives.

PUMP IT UP MAGAZINE: How can music heal and encourage women facing struggles?

CINDY DAVIS: Music connects emotionally, helping women feel understood, uplifted, and less isolated.

PUMP IT UP MAGAZINE: What challenges do you address through your music?

CINDY DAVIS: My music speaks from the heart, offering encouragement and hope to listeners.

PUMP IT UP MAGAZINE: How can women find strength in their faith?

CINDY DAVIS: True strength comes from trusting in God, staying prayerful, and believing brighter days are ahead.

PUMP IT UP MAGAZINE: How has music helped you overcome challenges?

CINDY DAVIS: A song by Ty Tribbett once lifted me from a dark time, reminding me of God's victory and hope.

PUMP IT UP MAGAZINE: What's your advice for pursuing dreams later in life?

CINDY DAVIS: Stay true to God's plan, keep praying, and never stop pursuing your goals.

PUMP IT UP MAGAZINE: How do you hope your music impacts others?

CINDY DAVIS: I want my music to inspire anyone who listens, leaving a lasting impact through themes of love, hope, and resilience.

Cindy Davis

PUMP IT UP MAGAZINE: How do Bible messages influence your music?

CINDY DAVIS: Love and forgiveness resonate deeply with me. The Bible's wisdom guides my music, emphasizing living a fulfilling life.

PUMP IT UP MAGAZINE: How does leading worship shape your connection with your audience?

CINDY DAVIS: As a worship leader, I aim to bring people into God's presence, which carries over into my artistry.

PUMP IT UP MAGAZINE: Can you share stories of women inspired by your music?

CINDY DAVIS: Before my broadcasting and music career, I led women's ministry and home Bible studies. I've witnessed many women find freedom and inspiration through the Word of God, and these stories continue to inspire my work.

PUMP IT UP MAGAZINE: How does social media help connect with audiences?

CINDY DAVIS: Social media enables instant engagement, allowing me to build a community and share faith messages globally.

PUMP IT UP MAGAZINE: How do you balance your roles while staying true to your mission?

CINDY DAVIS: prioritize my mission, pacing myself to avoid burnout, and staying focused on what matters.

PUMP IT UP MAGAZINE: What key lessons have you learned as an independent artist?

CINDY DAVIS: I've learned to manage my workload, prioritize what matters, and stay grounded in my mission.

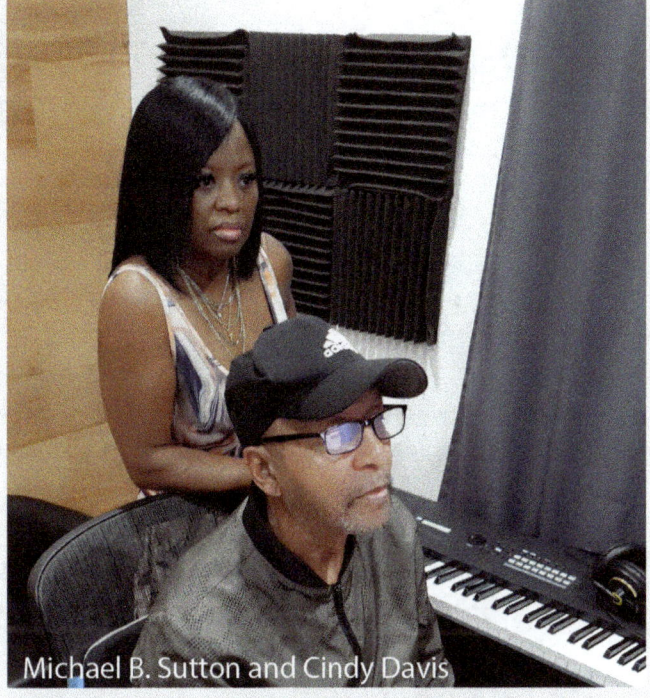

Michael B. Sutton and Cindy Davis

PUMP IT UP MAGAZINE: How does CinDav Productions align with empowering women?

CINDY DAVIS: CinDav Productions shares stories of women overcoming adversity, like Denise Matthews' transformation from fame to faith.

PUMP IT UP MAGAZINE: What's your hope for the next generation of female artists?

CINDY DAVIS: My vision is to spread messages of love, hope, and wisdom, inspiring others on their journeys of faith.

PUMP IT UP MAGAZINE: What's a key lesson you've learned from interviewing legends?

CINDY DAVIS: I've learned humility from legends like Freda Payne, who says, ***"If you've been doing something well for over 30 years, you are a legend.***

Photo by KoolShooters : https://www.pexels.com/photo/woman-in-pink-crop-top-and-jogging-pants-practicing-yoga-7346628/

DOPAMINE-BOOSTING WORKOUTS FOR A HEALTHY AND LONG LIFE

Boosting dopamine through exercise can improve mood, increase energy, and enhance well-being. Here's a simple routine for a healthier, longer life:

WARM-UP & STRETCH (5 MINUTES)
Start with a warm-up and dynamic stretches. This increases blood flow, prepares muscles, and signals your brain to release dopamine, setting a positive tone for your workout.

CARDIO BLAST (10 MINUTES)
Try high-intensity interval training (HIIT), jogging, or brisk walking. Cardio is proven to rapidly increase dopamine, boosting your mood and motivation. Short bursts of effort followed by rest can be effective.

STRENGTH TRAINING (10 MINUTES)
Do bodyweight exercises or lift weights. Moves like squats, lunges, and push-ups not only build muscle but also trigger dopamine release, making you feel more energized.

DANCE SESSION (5 MINUTES)
Put on your favorite song and dance! It's a fun way to elevate dopamine, relieve stress, and keep exercise enjoyable.

YOGA & DEEP BREATHING (5 MINUTES)
End with yoga poses and deep breathing. Poses like Child's Pose and Cat-Cow help relax your mind while boosting dopamine and serotonin.

NATURE WALK (5 MINUTES)
Fuel your body with a light, nutritious breakfast. Opt for something like oatmeal, fruit, or a smoothie to give you energy without slowing you down.

GET MOVING (5-10 MINUTES)
If possible, take a short walk outside. Natural light and fresh air further enhance dopamine production, promoting mental clarity.

Incorporate this routine daily to reduce stress, improve focus, and elevate your mood. Start small and stay consistent to enjoy a happier, healthier, and longer life!

TEST YOUR EMOTIONAL INTELLIGENCE: 8-QUESTION QUIZ

1. You receive unexpected criticism from a coworker. How do you respond?
A) Feel upset and take it personally
B) Ask for clarification and see if there's something you can improve
C) Ignore it and move on

2. How well do you recognize your own emotions as you experience them?
A) I often struggle to identify them
B) I can usually pinpoint what I'm feeling
C) I always know exactly what I'm feeling and why

3. You notice a friend is acting withdrawn. What do you do?
A) Wait for them to approach you
B) Ask them gently if they're okay
C) Assume it's not your business and move on

4. When faced with a stressful situation, how do you react?
A) I panic and feel overwhelmed
B) I take a few deep breaths and try to stay calm
C) I focus on solutions and maintain control

5. How do you handle disagreements?
A) I avoid them at all costs
B) I try to understand the other person's perspective
C) I get defensive and try to prove my point

6. You make a mistake at work. How do you handle it?
A) Try to hide it
B) Admit the mistake and focus on correcting it
C) Blame someone else

7. How well can you sense other people's feelings in social settings?
A) I rarely notice other people's emotions
B) I sometimes pick up on subtle cues
C) I am usually very aware of others' feelings

8. When dealing with stress, how do you maintain balance?
A) I often let stress affect my overall well-being
B) I try to balance stress with relaxation or exercise
C) I'm very good at maintaining balance even in tough times

SCORING YOUR RESULTS

Mostly A's: Your EQ might need some work. Focus on understanding your emotions and practicing empathy toward others.

Mostly B's: You have a decent level of emotional intelligence. Work on increasing self-awareness and managing emotions more effectively.

Mostly C's: You have a high level of emotional intelligence, demonstrating self-awareness, empathy, and self-regulation.

Wellness Secrets

Photo by Ylanite Koppens: https://www.pexels.com/photo/floral-ceramic-cup-and-saucer-above-open-book-1693626/

8 CHILL READS FOR STRESS RELIEF

Unwinding with a good book can be the perfect way to relax and find inner peace. Here are eight chill reads that provide an escape from everyday stress:

1. THE LITTLE BOOK OF HYGGE BY MEIK WIKING
This cozy guide explores the Danish concept of hygge—finding comfort in everyday moments. It's filled with tips on creating warmth and simple happiness.

2. BIG MAGIC BY ELIZABETH GILBERT
Gilbert's guide to embracing creativity is uplifting and freeing. It encourages readers to follow their passions without fear, making it a motivating read.

3. THE ART OF SIMPLE LIVING BY SHUNMYO MASUNO
Written by a Zen monk, this book offers 100 small ways to bring more calm into daily life. The advice is practical and easy to follow.

4. THE ALCHEMIST BY PAULO COELHO
This allegorical tale follows a shepherd's quest for his personal legend. It's an inspiring story of self-discovery that brings a sense of peace.

5. STILLNESS IS THE KEY BY RYAN HOLIDAY
This book combines philosophy, mindfulness, and timeless wisdom to show the power of stillness in a busy world.

6. THE BOOK OF JOY BY DALAI LAMA & DESMOND TUTU
This heartfelt conversation explores joy amid adversity, offering insights and practices to cultivate happiness.

7. CALM BY MICHAEL ACTON SMITH
This visually appealing book is filled with mindfulness exercises, quotes, and reflections that promote relaxation.

8. A MAN CALLED OVE BY FREDRIK BACKMAN
This touching story of a grumpy man finding love and friendship is heartwarming and uplifting. Enjoy these chill reads and let them melt away your stress!

Wellness Secrets

CHRISTIAN SONGS TO EASE STRESS & ANXIETY

PHOTO BY RDNE STOCK PROJECT: HTTPS://WWW.PEXELS.COM/PHOTO/BROWN-BIBLE-BOOK-ON-TOP-OF-PIANO-KEYS-8674215/

Music can be a powerful way to calm your mind and lift your spirit. Here are some uplifting Christian songs that bring peace, hope, and reassurance in times of stress:

"WAIT ON YOU" BY CINDY DAVIS
This song encourages patience and trust in God's timing, providing comfort and reassurance with its heartfelt lyrics.

"I'M GONNA BE READY" BY YOLANDA ADAMS
Yolanda's powerful vocals inspire listeners to prepare their hearts and minds, offering peace and strength to face life's challenges.

"GRAVES INTO GARDENS" BY ELEVATION WORSHIP
This uplifting anthem celebrates God's transformative power, bringing hope and renewal in uncertain times.

"JIREH" BY MAVERICK CITY MUSIC (FEAT. CHANDLER MOORE & NAOMI RAINE)
A song about God's faithfulness and provision, creating a sense of calm even when life feels unpredictable.

"BATTLE BELONGS" BY PHIL WICKHAM
With a message of surrender, this song encourages listeners to let go of their burdens, trusting God to fight their battles.

"GOODNESS OF GOD" BY BETHEL MUSIC (FEAT. JENN JOHNSON)
The song emphasizes God's enduring goodness, fostering gratitude and peace.

"RUN TO THE FATHER" BY CODY CARNES
This emotional song invites listeners to find refuge in God's love, offering comfort in times of stress.

"COME WHAT MAY" BY WE ARE MESSENGERS
An upbeat song that reassures listeners of God's constant presence, no matter the circumstances.

These contemporary songs offer peace, hope, and spiritual uplift for those facing stress and anxiety. **Listen to our Spotify playlist for more!**

Funk Therapy

| Funky | Trendy | Cool | Hip |

Wear The Music You Love!

Visit our merchandise store on our website:

WWW.FUNKTHERAPYMUSIC.COM

10% Discount code: STAYFUNKY

- Hoodies
- Crop Top
- Sweat Pants
- Bucket Hats
- Slides
- Mugs

UNISEX T-SHIRTS

Brown T-Shirt

GRAB IT NOW

Orange T-Shirt

GRAB IT NOW

Beige T-Shirts

GRAB IT NOW

Join our community
@funktherapy2

"Old School Party"
Funk Therapy feat. Michael B. Sutton

"'Old School Party' is my comeback anthem, thanks to therapy! Funk Therapy that is!

We may all have had some form of Therapy in our lives for one thing or another, yet music is the key to unlock **my true self.**
With the support of my beautiful wife Anissa Sutton and many others, she knew that music would be the key to heal and is my purpose on this earth - Reviving Souls with that Healing Power of that **Old School Music which we call Funk Therapy!**

I channeled new energy into recreating the 70's and 80s Funk-Disco- Soul - RnB - Magic I used to make for legends back in my Motown days. **Discovered by Stevie Wonder who led me to work at Motown**, I had the pleasure of working with some of the greatest, **Berry Gordy, Hal Davis, Michael Jackson, Smokey Robinson, Dionne Warwick, The Originals, Chuck Brown, Cheryl Lynn, Ray Parker Jr., Thelma Houston & Jerry Butler, Anita Pointer, Switch, and more....**

This song isn't just a tune; it's a throwback to the authentic '70s sound we all adore. Think good times, genuine vibes, and the heart of music. It's my way of inviting you to join the party, dance it out, and relive the joy we all miss!" **- Michael B. Sutton**

Single
"Old School Party"
Available
23rd February 2024

THE SOUND OF L.A.

PHOTO BY ALEXANDRA MARIA: HTTPS://WWW.PEXELS.COM/PHOTO/WOMAN-AT-SHOE-STORE-318236/

8 FASHION TIPS FOR OLD MONEY VIBES

Achieving the "old money" aesthetic is all about timeless elegance, quality, and understated sophistication. Here are eight fashion tips to help you exude those classic vibes:

1. CHOOSE QUALITY FABRICS
Invest in high-quality materials like cashmere, silk, and wool. These fabrics last longer and maintain a refined appearance.

2. STICK TO NEUTRALS
Embrace colors like beige, navy, cream, and soft pastels. Neutral hues create a polished, elegant vibe.

3. TAILOR YOUR CLOTHES
Well-fitted pieces are essential for an old money aesthetic. Ensure blazers, trousers, and dresses are tailored for a perfect fit.

4. OPT FOR CLASSIC SILHOUETTES
Go for timeless cuts like blazers, A-line skirts, and trench coats. Classic silhouettes never go out of style.

5. WEAR MINIMALIST JEWELRY

Choose simple pieces like pearls, gold hoops, or a delicate watch. Subtle jewelry adds sophistication.

6. SELECT TIMELESS ACCESSORIES
Structured handbags, leather loafers, or ballet flats complete the look. Opt for simple, elegant accessories.

7. KEEP MAKEUP NATURAL
Use neutral eyeshadows, light blush, and nude lipstick for a polished, natural look.

8. INVEST IN CLASSIC COATS
Choose outerwear like camel trench coats or wool overcoats. Timeless coats elevate any outfit.

Follow these tips to channel the refined elegance of old money effortlessly!

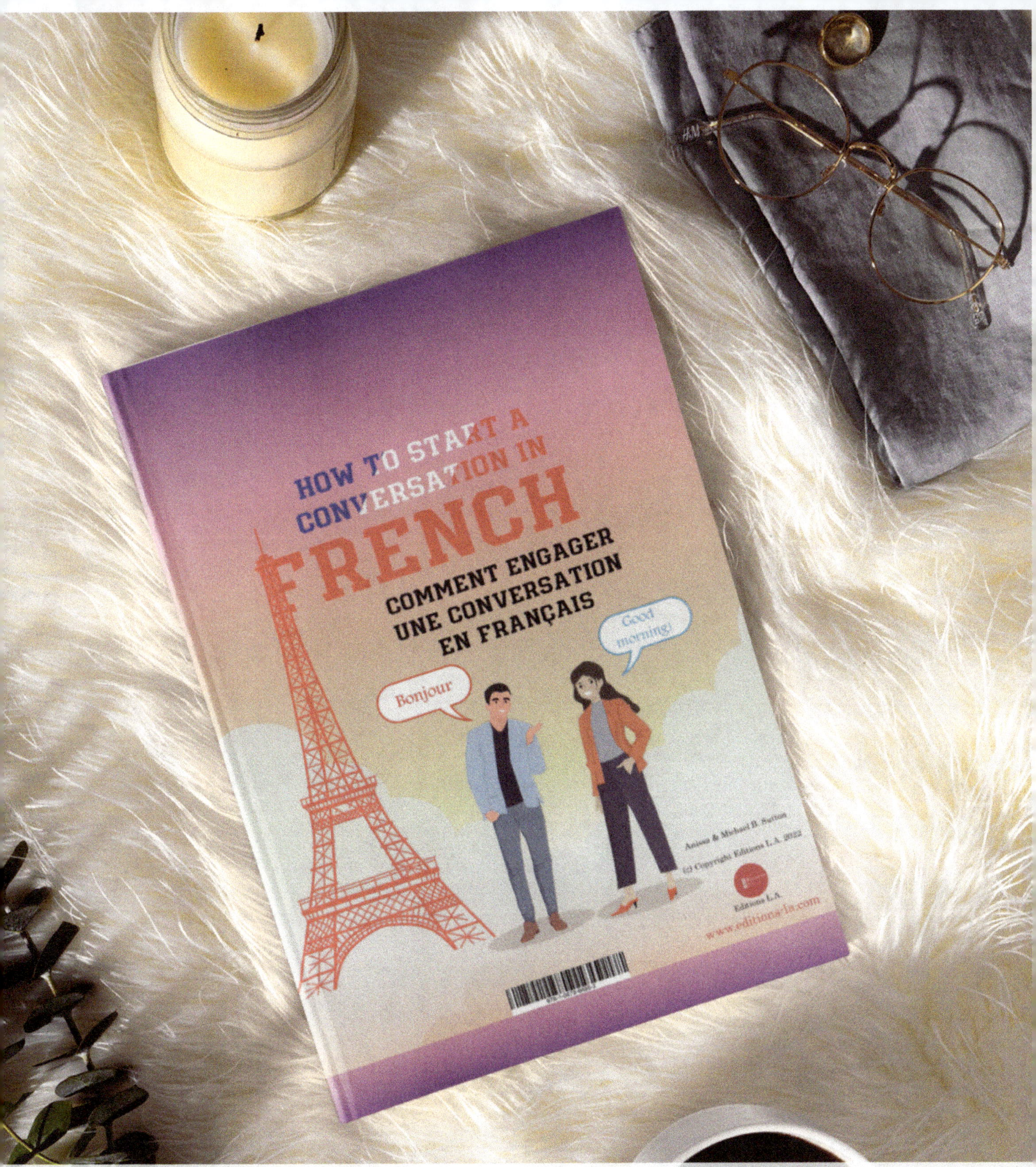
HOW TO START A CONVERSATION IN
FRENCH
COMMENT ENGAGER UNE CONVERSATION EN FRANÇAIS
Good morning!
Bonjour
Anissa & Michael B. Sutton
(c) Copyright Editions L.A. 2022
Editions L.A.
www.editions-la.com

Wellness Secrets

8 SLEEP HACKS FOR A BETTER YOU!

Photo by Pixabay: https://www.pexels.com/photo/woman-sleeping-on-mattress-covered-with-blanket-371109/

A good night's sleep is essential for a healthier, happier you. Try these eight sleep hacks to improve your rest and overall well-being:

1. SET A SLEEP SCHEDULE
Go to bed and wake up at the same time every day, even on weekends. Consistency helps regulate your body's internal clock.

2. CREATE A RELAXING ROUTINE
Wind down with a calming pre-sleep ritual like reading, meditation, or a warm bath. T his signals your body that it's time to sleep.

3. LIMIT SCREEN TIME
Avoid screens 30 minutes before bed. The blue light from phones and laptops can disrupt melatonin production, making it harder to fall asleep.

4. OPTIMIZE YOUR BEDROOM
Keep your room dark, quiet, and cool. Use blackout curtains, earplugs, and a fan to create the perfect sleep environment.

5. TRY RELAXING SCENTS
Use lavender or chamomile essential oils. These calming scents promote relaxation and better sleep quality.

6. LIMIT CAFFEINE IN THE AFTERNOON
Avoid caffeine after 2 PM. It can linger in your system, affecting your ability to fall asleep

7. STAY ACTIVE
Regular exercise helps you fall asleep faster and enjoy deeper sleep.

8. USE A COMFORTABLE MATTRESS AND PILLOW
Invest in quality bedding that supports restful, pain-free sleep.

EXPLORE
The World

WHY YOU SHOULD CONSIDER TRAVELING IN A MOTOR HOME

Freedom

When you travel with a motor home, you have the ultimate freedom to explore the world. You can go wherever you want, when you want and stay as long as you desire. No need to worry about finding a place to stay, looking for public transportation or dealing with airline tickets!

Affordability

You'll save money on accommodation since you'll be staying in your own self-contained living space. You'll also save money on food costs since you'll have a fully functioning kitchen in your motor home. Not to mention, you'll save money on transport as your motor home will get you from point A to point B.

Comfort

You will have access to a full kitchen, living area, sleeping quarters and bathroom, all in one vehicle. This means that you won't have to worry about packing up your things each time you move from one place to another. Plus, you don't have to worry about expensive hotel bills when you stay on the road for long periods of time.

BOOK NOW

- 123981 Craftsman Rd., Calabasas, CA 91302
- 1(818) 225-8239
- www.expeditionmotorhomes.com/

TRAVEL IN THE FOOTSTEPS OF JESUS: A SPIRITUAL JOURNEY THROUGH THE HOLY LAND

1. NAZARETH
Start in Nazareth, Jesus's childhood home. Visit the Basilica of the Annunciation, believed to be where the Angel Gabriel appeared to Mary, and explore nearby Nazareth Village, a recreation of a 1st-century village

2. SEA OF GALILEE
Head to the Sea of Galilee, where Jesus performed many miracles. Take a boat ride on the tranquil waters and visit Capernaum, known as "Jesus's own city."

3. MOUNT OF BEATITUDES
Reflect on Jesus's teachings at the Mount of Beatitudes, where He delivered the Sermon on the Mount. It offers a peaceful setting for prayer and meditation.

4. JORDAN RIVER
Experience a moment of renewal at the Jordan River, where Jesus was baptized by John the Baptist. Some sites offer the opportunity for visitors to renew their baptismal vows.

5. JERUSALEM
In Jerusalem, visit the Garden of Gethsemane, the Via Dolorosa, and the Church of the Holy Sepulchre, the site of Jesus's crucifixion and resurrection.

6. BETHLEHEM
Visit Bethlehem, the birthplace of Jesus. The Church of the Nativity marks the site of His birth, featuring a serene grotto that attracts pilgrims worldwide.

7. MOUNT TABOR
Experience the Mount of Transfiguration, where Jesus was transformed before Peter, James, and John. The panoramic views and Church of the Transfiguration make this a spiritually uplifting stop.

8. DEAD SEA
Take a detour to the Dead Sea, famous for its mineral-rich waters. While not directly tied to Jesus, it offers a place for relaxation and reflection.

9. BETHANY
Visit Bethany, home to Mary, Martha, and Lazarus. See the Tomb of Lazarus, where Jesus raised him from the dead, symbolizing hope and renewal.

10. QUMRAN CAVES
Explore the Qumran Caves, where the Dead Sea Scrolls were discovered. This site offers insights into Jewish history and biblical texts from Jesus's time.

11. MOUNT OF OLIVES
The Mount of Olives offers panoramic views of Jerusalem and is significant for Jesus's teachings and His ascension into heaven.

12. EIN KAREM
Explore Ein Karem, believed to be the birthplace of John the Baptist, and visit the Church of the Visitation, where Mary met Elizabeth.

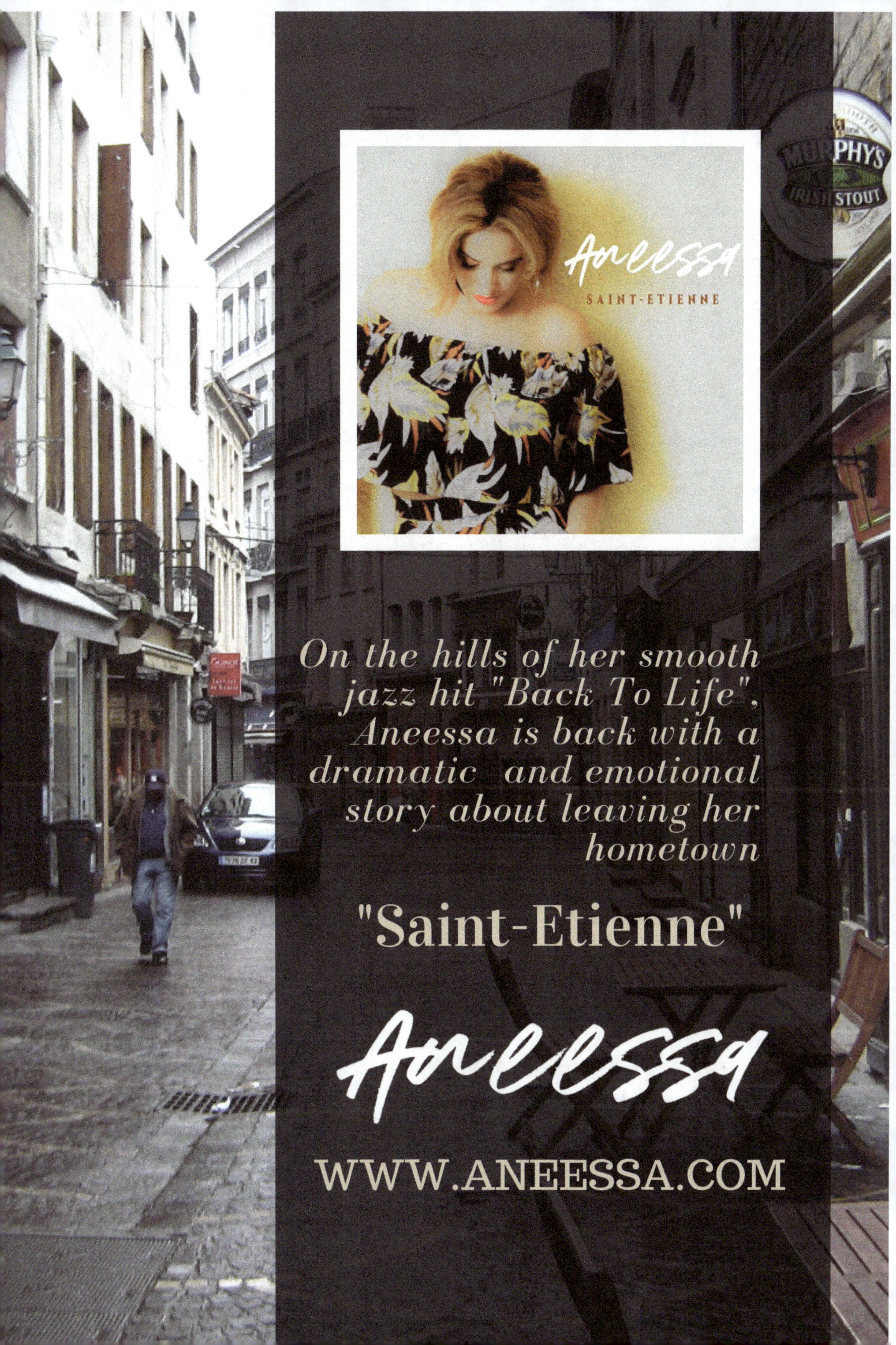

On the hills of her smooth jazz hit "Back To Life", Aneessa is back with a dramatic and emotional story about leaving her hometown

"Saint-Etienne"

Aneessa

WWW.ANEESSA.COM

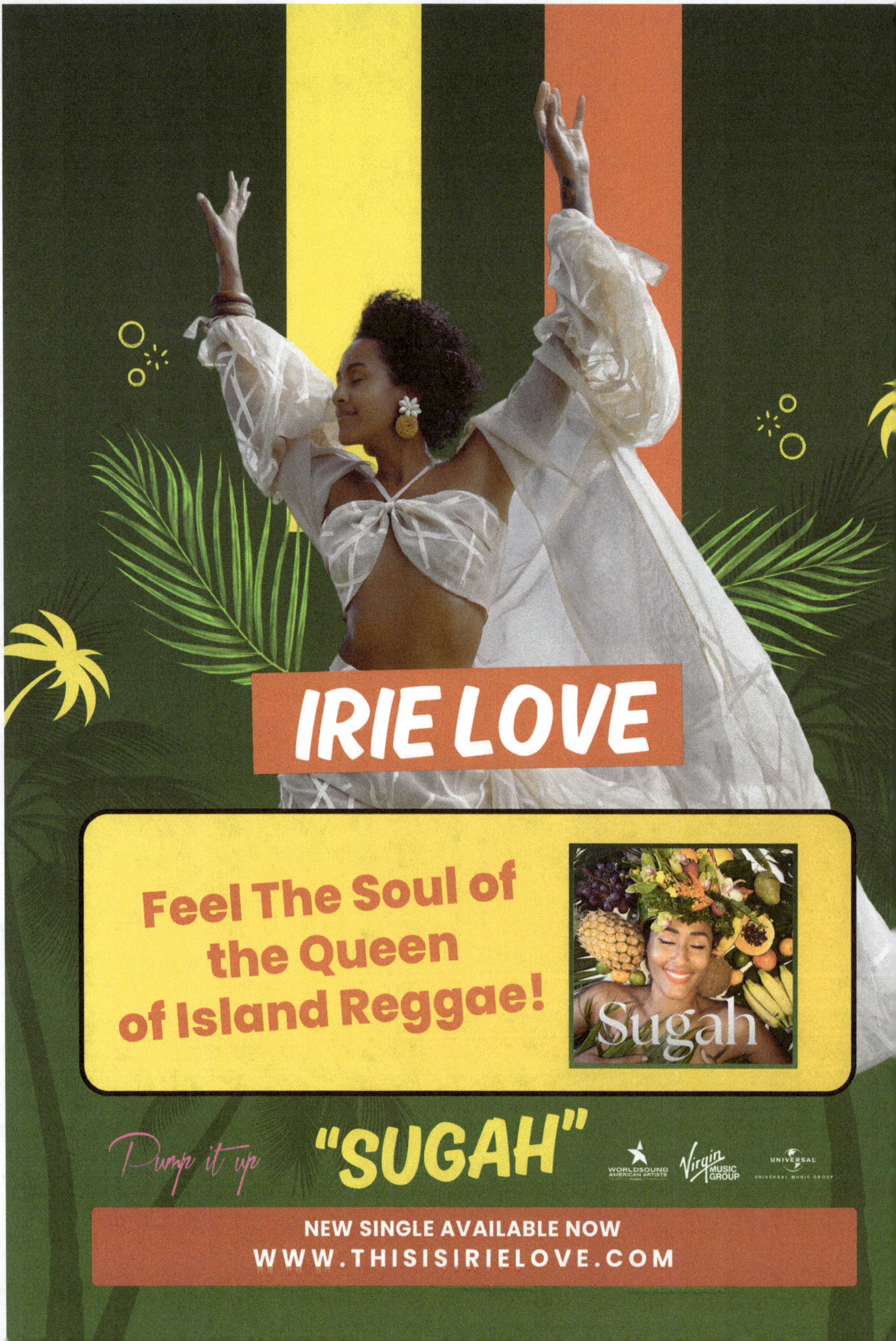

IRIE LOVE

Feel The Soul of the Queen of Island Reggae!

Pump it up **"SUGAH"**

NEW SINGLE AVAILABLE NOW
WWW.THISISIRIELOVE.COM

GLOBAL FREQUENCY
EVERYDAY 5PM (PST)
KPIU RADIO

LISTEN TO GLOBAL FREQUENCY EVERYDAY

HIP HOP - R&B - EDM

5PM - 6PM (PST) ON WWW.KPIURADIO.COM

HIP HOP - R&B - EDM
HOSTED BY GRANDMIXER GMS

KPIURADIO.COM

@KPIURADIO
@PUMPITUPMAGAZINE

SONG REQUEST
KPIURADIO.COM/DEDICACES-1

WWW.KPIURADIO.COM

WEST END ORGANIX

Ageless Beauty, Organic Health

Look and feel younger and healthier with our natural remedies products!

www.WestEndOrganix.com

Discount: 10% off of your order - Code *WEO2021*

Nonie
of Beverly Hills

Healthy Food for the Skin

Nonie of Beverly Hills™ is known best for its line of skincare products called AHA! Suitable for all skin types, these products are made from Alpha Hydroxy Acids and all-natural ingredients.
The range includes cleansing products, moisturizers for the face and body, sunscreens and shave cream.

Grapefruit seed extract is the only preservative used in the AHA! skincare line. AHA! products are made of all-natural plant oils, organic juices and plant protein containing no detergent, animal derivatives or by-products, mineral oil, alcohol, perfume, parabens or petrochemicals so they are excellent for vegans and vegetarians as well.

NONIE OF BEVERLY HILLS, INC, 812 SEWARD ST, LOS ANGELES, CA, 90038 USA

CONTACTS:
TEL: +323.467.1300 WEB: WWW.NONIEOFBEVERLYHILLS.COM
@NONIEAHA

Victoria Renée "A Better Tomorrow"

"A powerful & soulful voice, similar to Mariah Carey, Adele, Christina Aguilera, and Ariana Grande"

featured on CNN

From Indianapolis to LA, Victoria Renee Hand's musical odyssey started at 8, recording an album that charted in Europe.

Now a force in LA's music scene, Hand, mentored by Motown's Michael B Sutton and signed to The Sound of L.A., captivates with her soulful voice, drawing comparisons to Adele, Mariah Carey, Christina Aguilera, and Ariana Grande. Her track "A Better Tomorrow" featured on CNN showcases resilience, born from the Edie Hand Foundation.

Anticipate her upcoming album, "Secrets," dropping this summer. Join us on this sonic journey, one download at a time.

WWW.VICTORIARENEEHAND.COM

THESOUNDOFLA.COM

TOP NETFLIX MOVIES TO EMPOWER & INSPIRE

1. THE PURSUIT OF HAPPYNESS
Based on a true story, this film follows Chris Gardner's rise from homelessness to success. It's a powerful story of resilience, hope, and determination.

2. HIDDEN FIGURES
This film celebrates three African American women at NASA who broke barriers in the 1960s. It's a story of courage, intelligence, and the power of teamwork.

3. INVICTUS
This film tells how Nelson Mandela united South Africa through rugby, inspiring both the team and the nation. It's a lesson in leadership and reconciliation.

4. EAT PRAY LOVE
Based on Elizabeth Gilbert's memoir, this film explores a woman's journey of self-discovery and healing. It's about finding inner peace and embracing change.

5. THE BOY WHO HARNESSED THE WIND
The true story of a Malawian boy who builds a wind turbine to save his village. It's a tale of ingenuity, hope, and perseverance.n.

6. SELF MADE: INSPIRED BY THE LIFE OF MADAM C.J. WALKER
This biopic follows the journey of Madam C.J. Walker, the first female self-made millionaire in America. It's a story of ambition and breaking barriers.

7. THE THEORY OF EVERYTHING
The inspiring story of physicist Stephen Hawking, his struggles with ALS, and his groundbreaking work in science.

8. THE SOCIAL DILEMMA
A thought-provoking film that challenges viewers to rethink social media's impact, empowering them to make informed decisions..

9. LION
A heartwarming true story of a boy lost in India, adopted in Australia, who later searches for his birth family. It's a tale of determination and love.

10. JULIE & JULIA
Follows the journey of Julia Child and a modern-day blogger, celebrating passion, persistence, and pursuing dreams.

11. THE QUEEN'S GAMBIT
A story of a young orphan who rises to become a chess champion. It highlights empowerment, intelligence, and overcoming obstacles.

12. FREEDOM WRITERS
The true story of a teacher who inspires her at-risk students to find their voices and change their lives through writing.

13. MIRACLE
Based on the true story of the 1980 U.S. Olympic hockey team's journey to victory, it's a story of determination, teamwork, and overcoming the odds.

Reach for the stars, while standing on earth!

Angie Alley | Dr. Maya Angelou | Tahiera Monique Brown | Dr. Anne Bishop | Sunny Brown | Colonel (Ret) Jill Chambers | Linda Coons | Dr. Jan Davis, Astronaut | Vicki Drummond & Family | Krystal Drummond

Jan DuPlain | Mary Jean Eisenhower | Colleen Eikmeier & Family | Brenda Epperson Moore | Shelia Erwin | Charlotte Flynt | Dr. Suzanne Garber | Alie B. Gorrie | Victoria Hallman | Victoria Renee Hand

  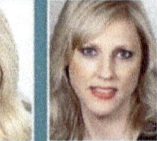  

Gemma Holmes | Conroy Kanter | Beverly Keel | Debby Keener | Lori Kelley | Sevetlana Kim

EDIE HAND'S
WOMEN OF TRUE GRIT™

PASSION • PERSEVERANCE • POSITIVE PROJECTION

60 + Heart moving stories of women from all walks of life who navigated with Grit to transform their lives and those of the people around them

EDIE HAND

Poem by Dr. Maya Angelou | Foreword by Bobbi Wells of American Airlines

Dr. Bobbie Knight | Dr. Judy Kuriansky | Kelly Lang | Tawana Lowery

Irlene Mandrell | Dr. Mary T. Maynard | Misha Maynard | Dr. Trevy McDonald

Carolyn McDonald | Dr. Shelia Nash-Stevevenson | Shirley Mullally | Cathy Nakos | Judy Nelon | Ellen Potts

Patsy Riley | Donna Roberts & Family | Lauren Robinson | Dr. Kimberly Robinson | LuLu Roman

Zsila Sadighi, M.D. | Jeannie Seely | Dale Smith-Thomas | Donna Stoney | Victoria, Edie & Linc Hand | Christy Joy Carlson-Swaid | Terre Thomas | Leigh Anne Tuohy | Shea Vaughn

Meredith Viera | Brigadier General (Ret) Wilma Vaught | Rhonda Vincent | Paula Moser Wallace | Dr. Lisa Watson-Morgan | Bobbi Wells | Jana & Mary White | CeCe Winans | Lady DiDi Wong

www.Pumpitupmagazine.com – www.EdieHand.com

HUMANITARIAN AWARENESS:
8 WAYS TO HELP STOP THE WAR AND SUPPORT THOSE IN NEED

War affects millions, causing devastation and displacement. Your actions can make a difference. Here are eight ways to help stop wars and provide support to those affected, with links for direct action:

1. DONATE TO TRUSTED HUMANITARIAN ORGANIZATIONS
Support global efforts by donating to:
International Red Cross – Provides emergency aid, medical care, and supplies in conflict zones.
Website: www.icrc.org
UNHCR – Helps refugees with shelter, food, and healthcare.
Website: www.unhcr.org
Doctors Without Borders (MSF) – Offers medical support in war-torn areas.
Website: www.doctorswithoutborders.org

2. RAISE AWARENESS ON SOCIAL MEDIA
Share stories, news, and verified sources about ongoing conflicts. Follow pages like:
Amnesty International – www.amnesty.org
Human Rights Watch – www.hrw.org

3. SUPPORT PALESTINIAN NGOS
Donate to:
Medical Aid for Palestinians (MAP) – Offers medical care and relief services.
Website: www.map.org.uk
Palestinian Children's Relief Fund (PCRF) – Provides healthcare and education to children in need.
Website: www.pcrf.net

4. ADVOCATE FOR PEACE
Contact your local government to support peaceful solutions. Use platforms like:
Change.org – www.change.org
Action Network – www.actionnetwork.org

5. VOLUNTEER WITH RELIEF EFFORTS
Offer your skills to organizations like:
International Rescue Committee (IRC) – Provides emergency assistance, resettlement, and support.
Website: www.rescue.org
Mercy Corps – Engages volunteers in fieldwork and logistics.
Website: www.mercycorps.org

6. HOST FUNDRAISERS
Use platforms like:
GoFundMe – www.gofundme.com
JustGiving – www.justgiving.com
Raise funds for humanitarian causes and donate proceeds to trusted NGOs.

7. SUPPORT MENTAL HEALTH SERVICES
Donate to organizations like:
International Medical Corps – Offers mental health programs in conflict zones.
Website: internationalmedicalcorps.org
Project HOPE – Provides psychosocial support for survivors of war.
Website: www.projecthope.org

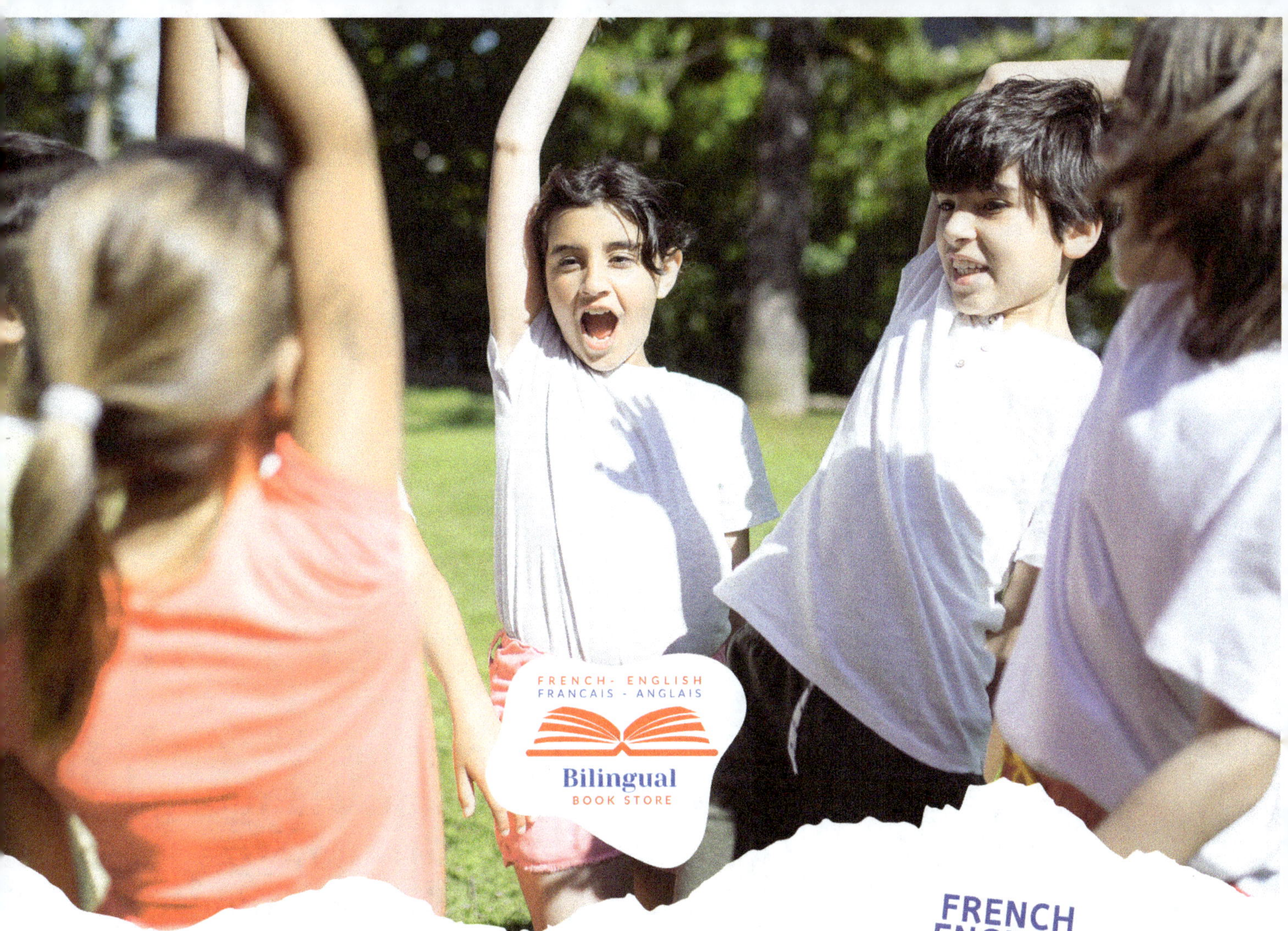

I AM - JE SUIS

AFFIRMATIONS POUR LA PENSÉE POSITIVE
AFFIRMATIONS FOR POSITIVE THINKING

Color & Learn French with Every Page!

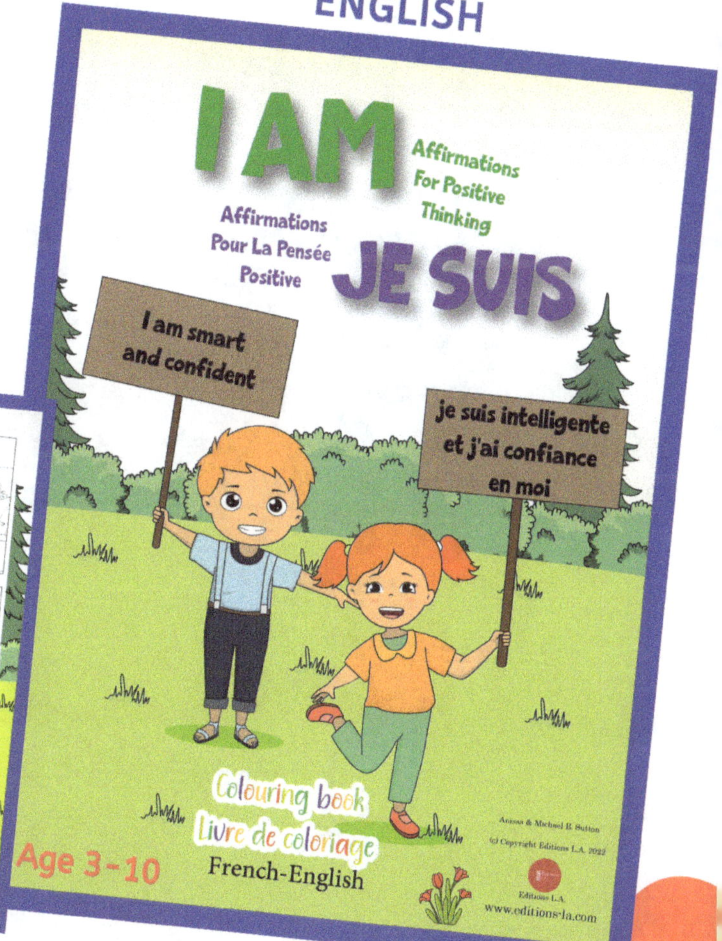

Benefits

- **Bilingual Skills:** Get a head start on French and English.
- **Positive Thinking:** Helps kids see the bright side.
- **Confidence Boost:** Full of confidence-building affirmations.
- **Fun Learning:** Who knew coloring could teach you a language?
- **Creativity Kick:** Boosts those creative and motor skills.
- **Smarter Every Day:** Sharpens memory and helps kids multitask.
- **Worldly Wise:** Opens up a world of cultures.
- **Family Time:** Perfect for some fun learning together.
- **Invest in the Future:** Sets kids up for success down the road.

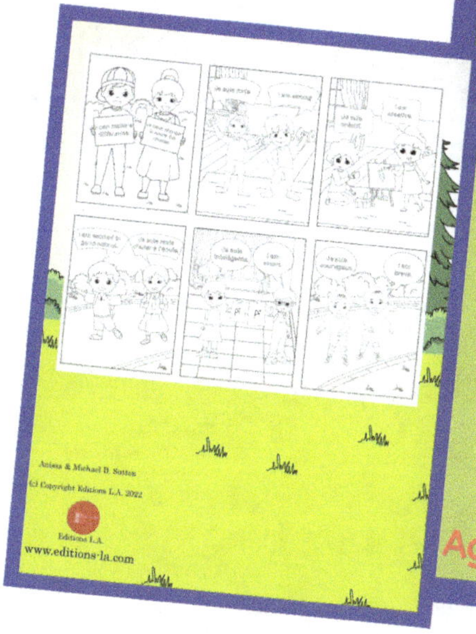

WWW.BILINGUALBOOKSTORE.COM

Easy French
FOR BEGINNERS

Tired of the struggle to learn a new language? Still traumatized by school teachers?

Don't let the past hold you back! Make learning French fun & easy with our bilingual books!

"EASY FRENCH FOR BEGINNERS" includes vocab, grammar, fun games, & quizzes.

SAY GOODBYE TO STRUGGLES AND HELLO TO FLUENCY! GET YOUR COPY NOW

nook   kobo   INGRAM   BARNES & NOBLE BOOKSELLERS    iBooks   amazon.com

 WWW.BILINGUALBOOKSTORE.COM